THE GIFT OF TEARS

COREY RUSSELL

D1493986

NASHARITE PUBLISHING

CONTENTS

OTHER RESOURCES FROM COREY RUSSELL

Corey Russell's heart is to bring together an online community of people from all walks of life who want to go deeper in the Bible and in prayer. To accomplish this, Corey is offering an online school where you can participate in many courses and view hundreds of teaching videos. Corey, along with occasional guests, offers three one-hour live sessions a month. Come join Corey and others in like pursuit at:

coreyrussellonline.com

Corey Russell has also written the following books:

Teach Us to Pray: Prayer That Accesses Heaven and Changes Earth

Inheritance: Clinging to God's Promises in the Midst of Tragedy

The Glory Within: The Interior Life and the Power of Speaking in Tongues

Ancient Paths: Rediscovering Delight in the Word of God

Prayer: Why Our Words to God Matter

Pursuit of the Holy

FOREWORD

LOU ENGLE

Bruce Wilkinson prayed the prayer of Jabez for thirty years after which he wrote the book, *The Prayer of Jabez*. Millions of copies were sold. It seemed the whole world was praying the prayer of Jabez. Was it Wilkinson's gift of writing and publication prowess that caused the book to fly? Partly, I would suppose, but I believe God set fire to the printed page and blew on it with His breath because, first, He desired the prayer to be globally prayed and, second, because thirty years of prayer and obedience moved His great heart to back up His man and his message.

"If I could use a pen as you can, I would write something that will make this whole nation feel what an accursed thing slavery is."[1] This was the exhortation given to Harriet Beecher Stowe by Mrs. Edward Beecher. Years later, President Abraham Lincoln met Stowe and said, "So this is the little lady who made this big war."[2] Stowe wrote *Uncle Tom's Cabin*, that little book that became the spark that ignited an abolition zeal that drove the nation into the great conflict that ended slavery.

Some books are written in ink, and some are written in blood, sweat, and tears before they're written in ink. *The Gift of Tears* has been written first in years of tears by the praying man, Corey Russell, a friend of mine and a friend of God's. Now we get to read the script.

I believe God will send fire on this book because of Corey's years of tears and tongues. I also believe *The Gift of Tears* could be catalytic in tipping the bowls of intercession in Heaven out of which the longed-for outpouring of the Spirit prophesied in Joel 2 will come. That is a pretty outrageous statement, and some would brand it rhetorical overreach, but doesn't Scripture and church history bear it out?

> "Turn to Me with all your heart, with fasting, with weeping, and with mourning. . . . And it shall come to pass afterward that I will pour out my Spirit on all flesh."
>
> — JOEL 2:12, 28

Evan Roberts, weeping for souls, cried out, "Bend me, bend me!" And the Welsh revival erupted. Frank Bartleman groaned and travailed in agony for revival for months and then Azusa Street exploded. One young man, one young woman reading this book could be gripped with this one thing, "I must get this kind of prayer!" Then after years of dying to self, he or she will reach that moment of Jacob's culminating crescendo cry that rips the veil, "I will not let You go until You bless me!" And then—revival!

God said, "I looked for a man!" (see Ezek. 22:30). Just one man. That is a statement of immense import, that God in Heaven would be looking for the weeping man, the weeping woman on Earth. This is not poetic fiction. God said to Daniel, the one who inaugurated a cosmic war in the heavens by mourning and fasting for twenty-one days, "O man greatly beloved!" (Dan. 10:19). And Jesus spoke concerning Mary that the memory of her perfumed tears would be spoken of through time and eternity (see Luke 7:47). *God, I pray, use this book, even this foreword, to find that man, that woman!*

1

TEARS THAT TENDERIZE

LIFE AS WE HAVE KNOWN IT FOREVER CHANGED IN 2020. A global pandemic shut everyone in their homes for most of the year. The sickness and death around us as well as the economic hardship from the lockdowns of businesses greatly impacted us all.

In the midst of the pandemic, a man by the name of George Floyd died while in police custody in Minneapolis, Minnesota. This event would awaken deep pain in the African American community and, in some ways, further the divide between blacks and whites in our nation. This moment would unleash rioting in the streets of America and give opportunity to militant groups to bring a lot of destruction to cities across our nation. It would also further the chasm as everyone ran to "their sides" to voice "their opinions."

On the back end of the year, we would enter into one of the most toxic, hate-filled election seasons in my lifetime.

Verbal wars between Republicans and Democrats, Conservatives and Liberals, filled our news channels, talk shows, and social media outlets nonstop, 24 hours a day, for many months. This season would climax on November 3, 2020, when an election that seemed to be pointing in the incumbent president's favor dramatically shifted through the night, and we would find over the next several days that a new president would be taking office in January of 2021.

The last months of 2020 and the first months of 2021 were around-the-clock banter on both sides, and this would come into the Church, creating division within her ranks. Many prophets boldly declared the sitting president would win a second term, yet when this did not happen, some of them repented while others continued on with, "Just wait and see."

What is God saying to us in these turbulent, confusing, and perplexing days? What is our call as the Body of Christ to a growing darkness in the culture?

As we see the divide grow and the pain become more filmed, expressed, and articulated, how do we respond when the turmoil in the Church is as loud as it is outside? What is the answer for days like these?

There are many ways to answer these questions, but this little book is a call to consider an often overlooked and neglected reality found in the Church: tears.

We need tears in this hour. I'm afraid that our hearts have slowly hardened over time without our realizing it. And it's made us unable to see, feel, and hear with hearts moved in the love of God for our world in our generation. More than likely, hardness of heart is the greatest threat to our ability to reach this generation with the gospel.

We are not a tender people, and because of this, our words, our lives, and our works are unable to pierce the hate-filled and polarized culture that we are living in.

Actually, this generation is not unlike many generations in the past. Other generations have experienced great division and animus. Thankfully, we've seen in those times how God awakens a remnant of people who come out of the chaos and trade in hearts of stone for hearts of flesh, enabling the Church to feel again, see again, and weep again.

The Lord made it very clear to Solomon in a dream that, when culture breaks down and darkness closes its grip on the people, it's a call to the people of God in that culture to go low, get tender, and humble themselves before God, seeking Him and asking Him to have mercy.

God promises to respond to such action by turning toward His people, hearing their prayer, forgiving their sin, and healing their land:

> When I shut up heaven and there is no rain, or command the locusts to devour the land, or send pestilence among My people, if My people who are called by My name will humble themselves, and pray and seek My face, and turn from their wicked ways, then I will hear from heaven, and will forgive their sin and heal their land. Now My eyes will be open and My ears attentive to prayer made in this place.
>
> — 2 CHRONICLES 7:13–15

Unless we humble ourselves, seek God's face, turn from our evil ways, and God moves, we are in deep, deep trouble.

Break Up Your Fallow Ground

Two hundred years after Solomon, the prophet Hosea gave a similar call to his generation when he likened their hearts to the ground outside and told them to do to their hearts what the farmer does to the ground every year.

> *Sow* for yourselves righteousness; *reap* in mercy; break up your fallow ground, for *it is time* to *seek* the Lord, *till He comes* and rains righteousness on you.
>
> — HOSEA 10:12

We must break up our fallow ground. The fallow ground is the hard soil that was useful in a previous season, but through weathering and time, it has become hard, immovable, weedy, and stony. The only way to make that ground useful again is to release the tiller and break it up, pulling up the soft soil below the surface and replacing the hard topsoil that won't allow any new seeds to be sown into it.

The book of Hosea is mostly a book of judgment as God is about to wipe out the northern tribes through the Assyrian invasion. Many times, Hosea asserted they were in a deadly cycle of judgment and were reaping what they had sown. They had plowed wickedness, and now they were going to reap iniquity. They had trusted in men and would find men unable to deliver them.

In the middle of Hosea's message of how they were reaping what they had sown, Hosea dropped this lifeline of a verse that in essence declared, "Israel, you can break the deadly sowing/reaping cycle by entering into a new sowing/reaping cycle."

- *Sow* for yourselves righteousness.
- *Reap* in mercy.
- *Break* up your fallow ground.
- *Seek* the Lord.
- *Till He comes* and rains righteousness on you.

One of the key phrases to me in this passage is *"for yourselves."* God has a part, and we have a part. God won't do our part, and we can't do His part.

Our part—regardless of what we feel, think, or sense—is to sow righteousness, break ground, and seek the Lord.

What does that look like?

In the simplest terms, it looks like individual and corporate prayer meetings, mingled with fasting, while asking God to forgive us as well as those we represent for our hardness, harshness, blindness, and deafness to Him and His ways. This also includes not neglecting compassionate works of love for the lost and broken around us.

I believe, while we seek to do this, God is going to release three gifts to us in these days to aid in the breaking up of our fallow ground:

1. Tears
2. Tongues
3. Travail

Revival Prayer

I believe with all my heart that 2020 and beyond will force the Church into a place of humility and brokenness that we have not seen for generations. We are leaving the station of well-polished, nicely articulated praying and are entering into the season of humble praying, broken praying, ugly praying. This kind of praying will provoke something in God to come and rain His righteousness on us.

Tears, tongues, and travail are coming to the Church. It's prayer on the other side of words, and this is what revival praying looks like. This is what it looks like when we've run out of words and nice ways to say something, and our eyes, our mouths, and our hearts scream, *"We need You, God!"*

I've labored for revival for over twenty years, and I'm finding that the longer and deeper my prayer life goes, the shorter my prayers become. I'm finding that I'm growing less concerned with how I pray something and more concerned over the place that I pray it from. I'm finding growing tears, sighs, and groans fill my prayer times, and although I don't know exactly what I'm saying, I know it's reaching God and He hears me.

This is revival praying. It's not about the eloquence of my articulation—or how theologically correct my prayers are—but it's how the depth of my soul reaches out to God in great desire for Him to move on my behalf.

We need tears. They are God's gift to us. The gift of tears is the outward sign of the inward revelation of our inability to change anything. They are the manifestation of poverty of spirit.

Tears are liquid prayer. They are liquid desperation.

Tears articulate the depths of our souls crying out to God, "I want You closer. I want You to rend the veil. I want You to come down. I want breakthrough in my family. I want breakthrough in my marriage, in my children, in my life, and in my nation. God, I need a breakthrough of You!"

God is not out to offend your pride. He's out to kill it. He's doing this to us on every level.

Earlier in Hosea, the Lord likened Himself to a Lion who will come and tear His people so that, in their affliction, they seek Him, and He returns and heals them. God said, "In their affliction, they will seek Me earnestly" (Hosea 5:15). I can't help but think the Lord is doing the same thing to us.

He is delivering us from respectability, arrogance, and self-sufficiency. God is bringing us to a deeper place of humility. He is allowing personal crises to bring forth a deeper prayer in us all. He will use personal issues in our lives, difficult dynamics in relationships, financial stresses, and anything else to get us past our nice, "Christianese" prayers—to get us into a deeper seeking and longing for Him. He means to break us out of our rigid religiosity.

I believe God is saying, "Let this moment cut you deeper. Let this trial have its work because I'm going to break in. I'm going to release a breakthrough, but you have to go through the waiting, through the cutting, through the breaking, through the death until the tears come, the travail grows, and the tongues are produced."

This isn't about emotionalism. I'm not just talking about tears of sorrow and woe. I'm not just talking about crying because of hard seasons. *I'm talking about tears that are a state-*

ment of our humanity, of our inability to make anything happen or bring about change. This is about a work of God in our souls, where He gets us to the place of human helplessness—to the place where we come face to face with our powerlessness. Whenever God brings us to this place where all our nice forms and words can't affect change, can't make anything better or different, in this place, tears start flowing. And these tears are a deliverance from our own righteousness. They are a language of the soul that's been brought to the end of itself.

Everything we've been through up to this point has been preparatory for the gift of tears to come, for a spirit of prayer to come, and for revival prayers to be released that lead to resurrection, breakthrough, and Holy Spirit outpouring. You and I can't manufacture this kind of crying and praying. No, because tears are a sovereign gift. They're a sovereign grace that God gives by the Holy Spirit to tenderize our hearts to receive the seed of the Word of God so that we can move into the next season.

As the prophet Hosea said, "It's time to seek the Lord." It's time to break up our fallow ground. It's time to break through the darkness of the hour. It's time to weep and groan and pray for revival in our generation . . . until He comes and rains righteousness on us.

Beloved, here in the pages that follow is a holy invitation for you into a place of prayer you've never been before—a place where *"deep calls unto deep"* (Ps. 42:7). The Father is calling us in this hour to the place where we run out of words, and He says, "Good." It's the place where we lean into Him and He gifts us with tears that move and provoke Him to show Himself strong on behalf of His people. Come, allow Him to anoint your eyes with fresh tears.

2

HANNAH'S TEARS AND JACOB'S WRESTLE

THE WORD OF THE LORD WAS RARE. THE priesthood was in shambles, and a generation had lost awareness of God. But it was in this hour that a barren woman came to the forefront. She is a prophetic picture of what God is doing in the prophetic Church across the earth.

God always births transitional generations through barren wombs. He did it through Sarah and the birth of Isaac. He did it through Rachel in the birth of Joseph. He did it through Samson's mom. He did it through Elizabeth with the birth of John the Baptist. And in Hannah's time, we see that Israel was in desperate need of a shift, so a barren woman came forward.

For years, Hannah refused to look at her barrenness. She enjoyed the benefits of being loved by her husband, of having a good life, and of being a good wife, but over time that wasn't enough to satisfy her heart. And then there was someone in her life whose very existence and capabilities of bearing children must have hurt her deeply.

The other wife in the story, Peninnah, began to provoke Hannah "severely," as 1 Samuel 1:6 tells us, "to make her miserable." We don't know exactly how she provoked her, but I have no doubt that there were many mean and hurtful conversations between the two. The other wife probably taunted Hannah, "Look at my life and look at yours. I'm able to give our husband children, and you aren't able to give him anything." Peninnah's verbal, hostile provocation seemed to go on for a while, and it grated on Hannah's soul.

Two times in the story, we read that "the Lord closed her womb" (1 Sam. 1:5–6). What do you do when God puts you in scenarios that He won't bail you out of until something breaks on the inside of you? God will allow external pressures to bring forth internal prayers.

Every year, the family would go to Shiloh to worship and to offer sacrifices. On this specific visit, something broke inside Hannah when the other wife started her provoking, and Hannah entered into a place of intercession that few in history have ever touched. *Her deep cries, tears, and travail will literally alter history.*

> So it was, *year by year*, when she went up to the house of the Lord, that *she provoked her*; therefore *she wept* [tears] *and did not eat* [fasting]. . . . And she was in *bitterness of soul* and prayed to the Lord and wept in *anguish*.
>
> — 1 SAMUEL 1:7, 10

Finally, the dam broke inside of this barren woman after all of the years of her not having children while the other wife had babies. And then what happened? What did she do?

She wept and didn't eat, and she was in bitterness of soul.

Hannah moved into one of the greatest prayers ever recorded. We see three important things in these two verses:

1. Bitterness of soul
2. Prayer
3. Anguish

For years, Hannah had run from the embarrassment, humiliation, and pain connected to barrenness, but in this prayer, she stopped running from everything and opened herself fully for God to see. And in such a condition, all she could do was pour out her heart before the Lord in anguish and bitterness of soul (see Ps. 62:8). Her vulnerability and humility penetrated the heavens and shifted history.

> Then she made a vow and said, "O Lord of hosts, if You will indeed look on the affliction of Your maidservant and remember me, and not forget Your maidservant, but will give Your maidservant a male child, then I will give him to the Lord all the days of his life, and no razor shall come upon his head."
>
> — 1 SAMUEL 1:11

One of the amazing things found in this prayer is that control was broken off Hannah. She didn't want a son so that she could showcase him to the other wife. She didn't want a son to shut everyone's mouth up. She didn't want a son to please her husband. Something had changed in her heart.

Hannah told God, "If You give me a son, I'll give him back to You."

Control was shattered, and Hannah declared that she would give her firstborn back to the Lord. No razor would touch his head, she vowed, which meant her son would be a Nazarite all the days of his life. He would fully belong to the Lord.

We don't want to overlook an informative part of her story as it testifies to both Hannah's manner of prayer and how a witness to her prayer reacted to it. We're told in verse 9 that Eli the priest "was sitting on the seat by the doorpost of the tabernacle of the Lord." And then we're told Eli watched Hannah as she prayed:

> And it happened, as she continued praying before the Lord, that Eli watched her mouth. *Now Hannah spoke in her heart; only her lips moved, but her voice was not heard.* Therefore, *Eli thought she was drunk.* So Eli said to her, "How long will you be drunk? Put your wine away from you!"
>
> — 1 SAMUEL 1:12–13

To me, verse 13 is one of the saddest verses in the Bible because the high priest didn't even recognize what the spirit of prayer looked like anymore. To Eli, this woman in desperation and crying out to God with tears and silent prayers looked like a drunk woman. The spiritual leadership of the day had completely lost discernment and no longer knew what true prayer looked like. *God, have mercy!*

Another thing that sticks out to me from this prayer is that it was silent. She *"spoke in her heart; only her lips moved, but her voice was not heard."* Arguably, one of the greatest prayers prayed was not even vocalized, which means her heart was screaming so loudly Heaven was moved!

We know the rest of the story. Hannah got pregnant very soon after this encounter and gave birth to a young boy and called him *Samuel*, which means "God has heard" as she had "asked for him from the Lord" (1 Sam. 1:20). Hannah gave Samuel back to God, taking him to live in the temple. At an early age, he was awakened by the Lord and was given a prophetic word that denounced the current spiritual leadership of Eli and his sons. Samuel continued ministering to the Lord in the temple, he grew up, and the Lord established him as a prophet, not permitting any of Samuel's words to fall to the ground (see 1 Sam. 3:19). And it was Samuel who anointed King David, whose very life would shift history forever. And it all goes back to a barren woman named Hannah.

Tears prevail with God when we're overcome by Him, friend, so let Him have His way with you and bring forth tears and a travail that alters history. Let Him take your anguish and release within you the spirit of prayer.

Prevailing with God

As we've seen in Hannah's story, the spirit of prayer is the anointing to prevail with God. The spirit of prayer is released when God has prevailed over us and brought us to a place of desperation just as He did with Hannah.

In Genesis 32, we find another person—another example for us—who had been brought to such a place. It was Jacob. He was returning to his homeland after having been away for twenty years. The last time he was home was just before he fled from his brother, Esau, after having stolen Esau's birthright.

For twenty years, Jacob had tried to steal a blessing. First, he had masqueraded as his brother to get the blessing from his father, Isaac. Then, he had tried to get the blessing of a perfect wife—the woman he loved—from his sneaky father-in-law. And that was a complete mess that included seven more years of hard work and marrying the woman's older sister. But now he was returning home and was unsure about what he would encounter. No doubt Jacob must have experienced anxiety whenever he thought about facing his brother. He must have wondered what kind of welcome he'd receive. So, it's not surprising that, upon entering his homeland and receiving word that Esau was coming out to meet him with 400 of Esau's men, fear gripped Jacob's soul. He began to divide up his wives and servants, sending them in different directions to divert and protect his entire family from being destroyed by his brother.

Evening came, and we read in Genesis 32:24, *"Then Jacob was left alone."* What a great verse! Stuff happens when you're left alone. When God backs you into a corner and gets you alone with Him, you're about to have an encounter that will change you forever. When He delivers you from all human ability, ingenuity, wisdom, and strength—from being able to do anything in and of yourself—God says, "Good. Now that I've got you alone and whittled down—now that you have no more solutions, no more ways to get yourself out of this situation—now that your greatest fears have come upon you, I'm going to lay hold of you, and I'm going to deliver you and transform you from Jacob to Israel. Now that I've got you backed into a corner, delivered from your own strength and know-how, I can use you."

Jacob's encounter is a great picture of what happens when God brings you and me to a place of desperation—a place where God lays hold of us to prevail upon Him! What will we do? Will we engage in prayer? Will we wrestle with Him for understanding and breakthrough?

Here's what Jacob did. Let's read the story:

Then Jacob was left alone; and a Man wrestled with him until the breaking of day. Now when He saw that He did not prevail against him, He touched the socket of his hip; and the socket of Jacob's hip was out of joint as He wrestled with him. And He said, "Let Me go, for the day breaks." But he said, "I will not let You go unless You bless me!" So He said, "What is your name?" He said "Jacob." And He said, "Your name shall no longer be called Jacob, but Israel; for you have struggled with God and with men, and have prevailed." Then Jacob asked, saying, "Tell me Your name, I pray." And He said, "Why is it that you ask about My name?" And He blessed him there. So Jacob called the name of the place, Peniel: "For I have seen God face to face, and my life is preserved." Just as he crossed over Penuel the sun rose on him, and he limped on his hip. Therefore to this day the children of Israel do not eat the muscle that shrank, which is on the hip socket, because He touched the socket of Jacob's hip in the muscle that shrank.

— GENESIS 32:24–32

When God gets you alone, and you don't have any other means of deliverance, that's when He lays hold of you. And when the revelation of what you've been made for collides with the revelation of where you're at, that's the vortex that pulls the groan out of the depths of your soul. That's where tears are awakened. That's where the wrestle with God happens—the wrestle that prevails with God and man.

God enabled Jacob to wrestle with Him so that He could bless Jacob with a name change and a breakthrough with Esau. This is what I want you to remember: *When God brings you to your breaking point, know that He is about to birth prayer in you and through you that will shift everything.* You will be changed forever, and you will no longer depend on the muscle that supported you in the past—the muscle of your human ability and strength. Instead, you will transfer the weight of your faith on Jesus, letting Him deliver, heal, and change your life.

Like Hannah and Jacob, I believe the Church is slowly coming to terms with our current state of barrenness and our powerlessness. In the past, we've run from our condition. We've tried to cover it. We've tried to come up with new strategies, yet to no avail. But I see the dam beginning to crack, and a new prayer is starting to rise within God's people. I believe one of the greatest prayer movements that the earth has ever witnessed is beginning to awaken within His people.

Humility, bitterness, tears, and anguish are beginning to well up, and they are going to erupt and shake the heavens. God is going to break control off of His people, and we will say, "God, give us sons and daughters, and we will put them before You in Your house! God, don't leave us where we are. We're not going forward until You bless us!"

3

MARY'S TEARS

FOUR DAYS LATE. THAT'S HOW LATE JESUS WAS. HIS dear friends Mary and Martha had sent a letter to Him, saying their brother, Lazarus, was sick. They knew Jesus had received the letter. They knew He had read the letter. And they knew He loved them deeply; they were dear to His heart. But the tormenting thought that had buffeted them for four days was, *Why didn't He come when He got the news?*

And why wouldn't Jesus come immediately to help His beloved friends?

Mary and Martha had to have been thinking, *Why didn't He just translate to Bethany, lay His hands on Lazarus, and then we would be celebrating something He had done so many times before for so many other people? If Jesus did this for strangers, then surely, He would do it for us, His close friends, wouldn't He?*

This part of the story begs the question: What do you do when Jesus hears your deepest groans, pains, and prayers but doesn't immediately respond to them?

You've been crying out to God for something, and He doesn't seem to move in accordance with your timetable. How do you respond when the thing that you've longed for the most dies?

I believe this furnace will either be the end of you, or it will be your breakthrough into the next season. When our nice theologies of the perfect Christian experience are destroyed, we are left with the choice either to withdraw our hearts and medicate our pain or live in the tension of what Jesus said He would do but hasn't yet done.

Something in the Process

We know from John 11 that, as soon as Jesus received the letter telling Him Lazarus was sick, Jesus made one of the most definitive statements in Scripture:

> *This sickness is not unto death, but for the glory of God, that the Son of God may be glorified through it.*

> — JOHN 11:4

Jesus didn't say Lazarus wouldn't die. He simply said the sickness wouldn't end in death. This is the thing that gets me: *Jesus knew what He was going to do from the very beginning, yet He still allowed the process of death to proceed and the pain of it to pierce His friends.* It makes me think there must be something in the process and not necessarily in the desired end that is useful to Him—that brings Him glory. Why does Jesus leave His friends waiting in their distress? Is there something in the delay that produces something necessary in their souls?

After all, Jesus didn't do this to a Pharisee, a Sadducee, or a stranger. He did this to His friends whom He dearly loved.

Today, if some of the things you have longed for have died, you are in good company. In fact, this is what Jesus does to His friends. Just ask Teresa of Avila.

While recounting a story of divine rescue in her autobiography, Teresa asked the Lord, "When wilt Thou cease from scattering obstacles in our path?" To which He responded, "Do not complain, daughter, for it is ever thus that I treat My friends." And she replied, "Ah, Lord, it is also on that account that Thou hast so few!"[1]

I'm convinced many of us in the Body of Christ have been in the exact same place as Mary, Martha, and Teresa. We have cried out to God to save a sick family member, to save ourselves, to save a fractured marriage, or to save a failing ministry, yet we haven't seen His immediate rescue.

How do we address this? How do we reconcile a good, compassionate, powerful God with the God who lets a loved one, a marriage, or a ministry die?

We need to slow down and look intently at this because our cheap, Christian phrases and clichés don't cut it. We've got to go deeper.

It's in this gap of four days that we see two types of responses emerge—one from Martha and the other from Mary. I believe most believers respond one of these two ways. It all really comes down to one question, though: Will you allow the fact that Jesus didn't show up in time to cut you or not?

Two Different Responses

On the outside, Martha appears to use all the right language and faith statements, but I'm convinced unbelief was below the surface of her glorified words, masquerading as faith. Let's take a closer look at the story.

John 11:20 tells us, "Then Martha, as soon as she heard that Jesus was coming, went and met Him, but Mary was sitting in the house." Note here that Martha went to Jesus *as soon as she heard*" He was coming. Interestingly, Martha never learned to sit and hear Jesus' words. She never learned how to come out of the swirl of distractions. She never learned to priest before the Lord so that, when the greatest crisis of her life came, she didn't know how to come out of it and sit before Him.

At an earlier time, before Lazarus fell sick and died, Jesus and the disciples had visited the siblings' house. Luke 10 paints the scene for us. Martha was in the kitchen working, busily attending to the needs of their guests, while Mary was absorbed in Jesus' words. Martha became distracted with much serving and completely missed the moment. She was annoyed by Mary's "laziness" and began to accuse Jesus of lacking empathy and fairness in His allowing Mary just to sit at His feet.

Jesus lovingly told Martha at that earlier time that she was worried and troubled by many things. *"But one thing is needed,"* Jesus had said, *"and Mary has chosen that good part, which will not be taken away from her"* (Luke 10:42). If Martha couldn't come out of the swirl when nothing bad was going on in her life, how was she going to come out of it when tragedy or difficulty hit? What was she going to do when she didn't understand what was going on or what to do about it?

That *"one thing"* Jesus was pointing out is the one thing for us all. If we get that one thing right, it will keep us in every season, especially seasons of great trial. But if we don't get that right, I'm reminded of Jeremiah's words to Israel, "If you have run with the footmen, and they have wearied you, then how can you contend with horses?" (Jer. 12:5).

The wisdom of Mary's choice would come to the forefront when these sisters would face the greatest crisis of their lives: the death of their brother. Wisdom is always justified later. For a while, wisdom doesn't look any different than anything else, but there will come a season that will cause wisdom to arise as wise and foolishness as folly. The five "wise" virgins of Matthew 25 cultivated oil, but for a season, they didn't seem any different than the foolish virgins. When the season began to shift, however, their wisdom emerged.

The story in John 11 is a case in point of this reality. Martha, when faced with the death of her brother and Jesus' unexplainable delay, had no history of waiting before Him; as a result, she was consumed once again with anxiety, worry, and trouble. I can see her pacing frantically in the house, reciting what she was going to say when Jesus finally showed up. I can hear her saying aloud, "Where were You, Jesus? Why didn't You get here?" The anxiety, anger, and swirl of the moment were too much for her soul, and she had no defense system; therefore, "as soon as she heard that Jesus was coming," she went to meet Him (John 11:20).

In contrast, every time we see Mary in Scripture, she is sitting. She sat in Luke 10 to hear Jesus' words. Looking once again at John 11:20, while Martha went to meet Jesus, we read "but Mary was sitting in the house." Mary was sitting in Luke 10, she was sitting in John 11, and she was sitting at the feet of Jesus, anointing Him with the oil from her alabaster box in Mark 14. Her sitting is the picture of a life surrendered to God. I believe this posture is one the Lord wants to emphasize in these days. There is *so much more* to this sitting than we realize.

Martha—filled with anxiety, frustration, and anger—will rush right into the doctor's office, wanting to get a problem resolved. But not Mary. Mary will wait in the waiting room to be called into the doctor's office. And that's the difference between their two responses.

Martha came to Jesus and said, "Lord, if You had been here, my brother would not have died" (John 11:21). That's the key phrase; in fact, it's the very same phrase that Mary will make to Jesus eleven verses later, but the place Mary prayed it from is massively different than the place her sister, Martha, prayed it from.

Martha continued, "But even now I know that whatever You ask of God, God will give You" (v. 22). At first glance, this prayer sounds as if it's filled with faith and confidence, but I'm convinced that it's not as awesome of a prayer as we think. There are a few reasons why:

1. She will use the phrase, "I know," twice. Usually, when someone has to say, "I know," a second time, they really don't know.
2. She asked Jesus to ask God, which meant she didn't see Jesus for who Jesus is.

3. Jesus' response to her will be a call to faith in the revelation of who He is.
4. Moments before Lazarus is raised from the dead, she will say he stinks since he has been dead for four days.

For these reasons, I believe her great prayer covered up her unbelief.

This entire interaction between Martha and Jesus is so vivid as Martha anxiously prayed, yet Jesus appeared unmoved by it. He made a clear, definitive statement about Lazarus—"Your brother will rise again" (v. 23). It seems that Jesus was calling Martha off the sidelines of her asking Him to ask God and looking to pull her into the story by her faith.

As soon as Jesus made this statement, Martha quickly rebutted, "I know that he will rise again in the resurrection at the last day" (v. 24).

Once again, Martha's theology was amazing as we see that she understood about the resurrection of the dead. It's great that she was looking to the future day when all the righteous rise from their graves. But Jesus was still looking to pull her faith into the story, to have her partner with Him in raising her brother from the dead. And that's when He said the most powerful words: *"I am the resurrection and the life"* (v. 25).

Resurrection isn't coming someday, Martha. Resurrection isn't coming someday, reader. That Resurrection is a Person, and He is standing right in front of you. He is looking for a faith that pulls "someday" into "today"!

Jesus is *the* Resurrection and *the* Life! I don't care how dead your life is, your marriage is, your children are, your family is, your finances are, your body is, your relationships are—*He is* the Resurrection and the Life. I believe He is showing up to His friends in this hour, and He is looking for more than pretty, perfect, correct prayers. Jesus is looking for a place of brokenness in our prayers, for prayers of brokenness move Heaven.

Let us learn from Martha and refuse to hide behind bumper stickers, T-shirts, and right phrases. Let the divine delay touch you and cut you, and then let it produce a cry that you've never experienced before.

Our ability to impact God with our prayers is directly connected with the divine delay's ability to impact us. If we refuse to let it touch us, we can have nice prayer times, grow in theology, and live at a distance from Him. But it won't move Heaven. Jesus wants something deeper.

Martha didn't get it. We read that, after she had her say, "she went her way and secretly called Mary her sister, saying, 'The Teacher has come and is calling for you'" (v. 28). I absolutely love this last line. Why?

Because I believe that Jesus is calling for Marys all over the earth who will come out of the waiting room of intimacy and wrestle through the confusion to partner with Him in seeing resurrection power released in their situations, families, cities, and nations. He wants us to partner with Him to release revival in the earth.

I want to highlight a couple of things here. First, we don't see recorded in Scripture that Jesus asked for Mary. What did Martha run into that caused her to realize she was not going to be able to get them out of this mess? Could it be that, because she didn't learn the first lesson in Luke 10 of waiting on Jesus, she was unprepared for her hour of trial?

Second, can you see the difference between Martha and Mary in regard to Martha running out to Jesus and Mary waiting for the invitation? I can't help but think again of a doctor's office and how the only way you can get to see the doctor is by "waiting in the waiting room." After all, it's called a *waiting room* for a reason. You must first wait before you are called.

Mary was called, but Martha barged in.

Martha went to see Jesus as she heard Jesus was coming, but Mary went to see Jesus only after He called for her. And when Mary got to Him, "she fell down at His feet," and said to Him, "Lord, if You had been here, my brother would not have died" (John 11:32).

What? Mary spoke? Did you know this is the only recorded statement attributed to Mary in Scripture?

Mary basically repeated what Martha had said when Martha went out to meet Jesus. But when Mary said it, she said it having fallen at Jesus' feet, and she said it while *weeping*. What we witness in verses 21 and 32 is how two people can pray the exact same prayer yet pray it from two completely different, physical postures as well as two completely different, heart postures.

Where Martha made her initial statement backed up with her two "I know" statements, Mary made her statement inter-mingled with tears at Jesus' feet. Martha said she knew. Mary didn't understand. "Jesus, I don't understand why You didn't get here sooner. If You had, my brother wouldn't have died. I don't understand, Jesus."

Have you ever been in this place? Are you in this place now?

Have you had a marriage that you've cried out desperately to Jesus for, and it seems that things have only grown worse? "Lord, if You'd been here, my marriage wouldn't have died."

Have you raised a son in the things of the Lord only to see him run far away from God in his teenage years? "Lord, if You'd been here, my son wouldn't have run off to Stupidville and gotten his life all messed up."

Have you been a faithful tither and giver and yet seen your finances depleted? "Lord, if You'd been here, my finances wouldn't have all dried up."

Martha said this, and then she tried to clean it up with her good theology and Christianese. She wasn't letting the divine delay cut her. And many of us refuse to let the delay cut us, but Mary let it cut her.

Jesus is looking to produce something in us. I'm convinced He is delivering His people from pretty prayers and taking us into ugly praying. The ugly prayers are guttural responses to the divine delay—to the "I don't know what's going on. I don't understand why Jesus hasn't come yet. Why isn't He answering me?" They're the prayers that gush out from our souls. They're the raw reactions to the cutting. They're the prayers wrought with the wrestle of confusion and disillusionment—of not understanding why Jesus hasn't broken in when all along He could have.

I'm convinced that God is bringing the Church to a place of prayer on the other side of words. It's a place of brokenness, humility, and desperation that is going to usher in words, prayers, and actions that penetrate the heavens and hearts of men and women in our noise-saturated culture.

I believe tears are coming to the Church. It won't be mere emotionalism or striving and religiosity, but a gift of tears. This gift is the revelation of our inability to change anything in and of ourselves.

Tears flow where solutions cease. Mary fell at Jesus' feet in the swirl of confusion, not knowing or understanding why He delayed. She let that cut into her, and she wept.

I believe Mary sat at Jesus' feet in the past and allowed His words to go to her deep so that, in the hour of her crisis, her deep called out to His deep, and it pulled a resurrection out of Him.

4

"JESUS WEPT"

WHAT DOES IT TAKE TO MOVE GOD'S HEART? WHAT stirs up His passion to perform a miracle, to intervene on the behalf of His friends? What pulls a resurrection out of Him?

Mary of Bethany knew how to move Jesus. She knew how to stir the bowels of mercy of the King of all nations. Her brokenness, her falling to His feet and weeping, that's what cut Him—to the point that it says, "He groaned in the spirit and was troubled" (John 11:33).

I wonder what that looked like. What kind of prayers cause God to groan? Think about that.

Do you want to trouble God—to cause Him to groan in the spirit? Do you know you can? You can stir Him. You can ignite His compassion to interject Himself into your situation, your family, your church, your city, your nation, and your world. That's what Mary did.

The groan caused Jesus to ask the mourners who had followed Mary, "Where have you laid him?" (v. 34).

I believe Jesus waited the four days and let the process play out so that He could bring His friends to this place of prayer—to this place where Jesus' spirit was provoked to groan. As we see from the beginning of this story, Jesus knew how this was going to end. It was going to end with Jesus being glorified and not end in the death of His friend.

Jesus let this story unfold, let the responses come, and the process play out because He was looking for something. He was looking for someone to pull something out of Him, to partner with Him in the resurrection of Lazarus. And He found it in Mary, the one who consistently sat at His feet.

I don't know how you read this story of Lazarus being raised from the dead, but to me, everything up until this point seems to move quickly. It may have been four days of arduous waiting for Mary and Martha, but for us readers, things are clipping along:

- The sisters send a letter to Jesus.
- Jesus reads the letter.
- Jesus tells His disciples the sickness won't end in death, but He will be glorified in it.
- Jesus stays away a couple of days.
- Suddenly, Jesus tells His disciples that Lazarus is dead.
- Jesus and the disciples go to Bethany.
- Martha hears Jesus is coming and rushes out to meet Him.
- They have their conversation.
- Martha comes to Mary and tells her Jesus wants to see her.

- Mary goes to meet Jesus and falls at His feet, weeping.
- They have their conversation.
- Jesus asks where they have placed Lazarus.
- The mourners tell Jesus to "come and see" (John 11:34).

Stop!

Everything seems to stop when we read the next verse, verse 35. It's the shortest verse in the Bible, but it actually seems the longest. Why? Because surrounded on every side by skeptics, critics, strangers, disciples, and friends, time stops as the Son of God—the Creator of Heaven and Earth, the Uncreated One, the Ruler of the nations, the King of all kings, Jesus —does the unthinkable: He weeps.

"Jesus wept."

This is holy. Put down your clipboards of dissection and analysis and watch Him weep. It's holy ground. Connect with the fact that the God who created everything—the One who "measured the waters in the hollow of His hand, measured heaven with a span" is weeping (Isa. 40:12).

See these two words in verse 35 as Charles Haddon Spurgeon saw them, who wrote:

> I have often felt vexed with the man, whoever he was, who chopped up the New Testament into verses. He seems to have let the hatchet drop indiscriminately here and there; but I forgive him a great deal of blundering for his wisdom in letting these two words make a verse by themselves: "Jesus wept." This is a diamond of the first water, and it cannot

have another gem set with it, for it is unique. *Shortest of verses in words, but where is there a longer one in sense?* Add a word to the verse, and it would be out of place. No, let it stand in solitary sublimity and simplicity. You may even put a note of exclamation after it, and let it stand in capitals,

"JESUS WEPT!"

There is infinitely more in these two words than any sermonizer, or student of the Word, will ever be able to bring out of them, even though he should apply the microscope of the most attentive consideration. "Jesus wept." Instructive fact; simple but amazing; full of consolation; worthy of our earnest heed. Come, Holy Spirit and help us to discover for ourselves the wealth of meaning contained in these two words. [1]

For years, I thought it was a mere slipping of a tear, a sniffle, or a brief moment of emotion, but I've begun to see that, at this moment, a storm formed in Jesus' spirit and came raging out in torrents of tears. *Jesus wept.*

Jesus heaved and cried and sobbed. And we must stop and watch Him weep. We can't move on so quickly to the next verse. We have to behold the weeping God in all of His vulnerability as He gathers up all the pain, sorrow, accusation, and plots of wicked men and weeps in front of us all. *Jesus wept.*

I believe Jesus hates death so much that He was weeping over the curse of death and what it had done to His friend. And He was about to abolish it in front of everyone there. But you can't just run to the resurrection of Lazarus. You have to get in the valley of weeping with Jesus. We have to go to the valley of tears because that's the place from which resurrection manifests. We must stop here and watch *Jesus as He wept*.

We're a generation that wants to translate right to the resurrection, but it's as if God is saying, "Whoa! You're going to find Me in the brokenness, in the weeping." There's a place of humility, vulnerability, and honesty. There's a place where all of your views of God are put to the test. This is the place where you wrestle with how you really feel. And this is where faith arises in your heart.

Faith doesn't look like false confidence. Faith cries out, "God, I don't understand! I'm going to let this go deep, and I'm going to get ugly with You, God, because I want reality."

And that's what Jesus was responding to in Mary. He wept, and His tears were tears of deep compassion for Mary and Martha. These were tears of deep sorrow for humanity. These were tears of deep love for Lazarus. These were tears of deep anger for the Pharisees who were plotting His death. These were tears of deep hatred for death and what it steals from humanity.

Whoever says, "Men don't cry," read this verse: "Jesus wept!"

Only a Weeping God Can Wipe Away Our Tears

I sense the Holy Spirit inviting the Church into a new place. It's called the *weeping room*. This room is a place in the heart of God where the divine emotions are imparted and shared with His people. Our ability to let Him be vulnerable with us, thereby allowing us to be vulnerable with Him, is going to release resurrection power in our lives, families, and circumstances.

Several times in the Revelation of Jesus, we see that God Himself will come and personally address our tears, wiping them away. How close does God have to be to wipe away our tears?

On January 23, 2016, I had an encounter with Jesus, where I sensed Him walk into my living room, get down on His knees, and ask for permission to shepherd me and minister to me. In that encounter, He led me to Revelation 7:17.

> "For the Lamb who is in the midst of the throne will shepherd them and lead them to living fountains of waters. And God will wipe away every tear from their eyes."

Here, God ministers to those who have just come out of the tribulation. This not only applies to those who come out of the Great Tribulation at the end of the age, but also applies to those who have walked through tribulation seasons in this life and are in need of ministry from God.

God wants to come into our valleys of weeping today. He wants to apply that same ministry. He wants to come close to you, to take His thumb and wipe away the pain and trauma of this age. And He is asking you what He asked me in 2016, "Will you let Me shepherd you? Will you let Me minister to you?"

Beloved, only a weeping God can wipe away our tears. Only a weeping God can bring resurrection life to us.

Tears and Resurrection Are Connected

After this time of weeping, Jesus began to move toward the tomb. He groaned again in His spirit. Can you hear the groan? Can you see Him? He was still wiping away His tears before moving into resurrection mode.

Jesus arrived at the tomb. "It was a cave, and a stone lay against it" (John 11:38). And He said, "Take away the stone" (v. 39). Here was the moment that, though Mary and Martha may not have realized it, they had been waiting for. Jesus' zeal was about to be released in a breakthrough miracle. I mean, resurrection power was about to explode, and Martha had to say something: "Lord, by this time there is a stench, for he has been dead four days" (v. 39).

Now, you see why I was so hard on Martha. Because here was the real Martha. She was showing her true colors. Her statement exposed her lack of faith, proving to us that all her alleged faith-filled comments earlier in the story were not what they seemed to be. I love Martha. Jesus loved Martha, but she didn't get it. And Jesus refused to let her off the hook. He said, "Did I not say to you that if you would believe you would see the glory of God?" (v. 40).

Then some of the ones standing by removed the stone. And Jesus, lifting up His eyes, said, "Father, I thank You that You have heard Me. And I know that You always hear Me, but because of the people who are standing by I said this, that they may believe that You sent Me" (vv. 41–42).

One of the greatest secrets to authority in prayer is found in the living awareness that the Father hears us. His ears are open to His children, His heart is engaged, and His hand is ready to move.

Do you believe that your Father in Heaven hears you when you pray?

Jesus did. And after He had "said these things, He cried out with a loud voice, *'Lazarus, come forth!'* And he who had died came out bound hand and foot with graveclothes, and his face was wrapped with a cloth. Jesus said to them, *'Loose him, and let him go'*" (vv. 43–44).

The great warrior God released His roar! And he who had been dead for four days came out of the grave! Then those around Lazarus freed him from his graveclothes. And the revelation of the resurrection by God was made manifest for everyone to see.

Friend, Lazarus is coming out of the tomb in this season. As we come into the weeping room with Jesus and go to a new place of vulnerability and tears, we are going to see a resurrection roar released out of our lives that will literally witness the resurrection of spouses, children, finances, bodies, and churches. We will see personal resurrections, marriage resurrections, family resurrections, financial resurrections, healing, deliverance, and breakthrough in the places for which we've cried out for years for God to move.

We are going to see a mighty spirit of revival hit this nation, and we will see a generation that had left the Church and gone deeply into the world begin to supernaturally come back. I'm feeling even as I write this that we are in a divine window where Jesus is inviting us into the weeping room, and out of this season one of the greatest revivals that has ever been released upon the earth will come. In the same way Lazarus's resurrection sparked the plotting of Jesus' death, so I believe that the resurrection power that is about to be released upon our nation and the globe will provoke a great rage that will set the stage for the second coming of Jesus.

Tears and resurrection go hand in hand. We witnessed it in our story here. Jesus wept, and Lazarus was resurrected. And we see it in Jesus' death and resurrection. Hebrews 5:7–9 tells us that Jesus, "when He had offered up *prayers and supplications, with vehement cries and tears* to Him who was able to save Him from death . . . became the author of eternal salvation" for us. His tears and resurrection sealed all of ours! Not only ours, however, but Israel's future resurrection. Luke 19:41 recounts to us how Jesus saw Jerusalem "and wept over it." Romans 11:15 tells us that Israel's acceptance will be "life from the dead."

God is imparting the gift of tears to His people in this hour. This gift is not manipulated, worked up, or earned, but it's a divine grace. It's born out of human inability to make anything happen. I promise you that God will whittle you down to a place of dependence, humility, and brokenness. And this place is where prayer begins. It's the kind of prayer that penetrates, reaches, and breaks through.

Tears come when you run out of options. They are a language all their own. They're the expression of a soul that's on the other side of words. Such tears will provoke a response in God. He won't be silent at your tears (see Ps. 39:12).

God is taking us to a deeper place of prayer, and tears will accompany the spirit of prayer.

5

WEEPING PROPHETS AND APOSTLES

MY JOURNEY WITH THE GIFT OF TEARS BEGAN IN 2002. My family and I had moved to Kansas City, Missouri, in December 2000 to join a new ministry called the *International House of Prayer* (IHOP). We were serving as "intercessory missionaries" and were loving all that God was doing in our lives.

One morning when I was in the IHOP prayer room, a friend came to me and told me that God was about to make me a watchman like Jeremiah. I honestly had no clue what he meant, but I was intrigued by it. I didn't have any grid then for Jeremiah outside of the famous verse:

> For I know the thoughts that I think toward you, says the Lord, thoughts of peace and not of evil, to give you a future and a hope.
>
> — JEREMIAH 29:11

The next morning, I woke up early and decided to read the book of Jeremiah and see what God would say to me as I read it. From the moment that I opened the book, I experienced something that I had never experienced before in my life. I began to weep as I read through the book. Tears began to flow through my eyes, and I knew I was experiencing a baptism into tears.

I began to see the similarities between Jeremiah's day and the day we are currently living in. I began to see the disconnected spiritual leadership, the lack of prophetic discernment from the prophets, and the overall ease that had settled in on people.

The Weeping God

For the next three days, I would read Jeremiah over and over again just weeping. Honestly, eighteen years later, the weeping hasn't stopped. Most mornings when I first wake up and open my Bible, I begin to weep. I don't fully understand it, but I know it's tenderizing my heart and my spirit, as well as preparing me for the spirit of revelation to hit me.

It was in this initial encounter where the Lord spoke to me about Jeremiah. The Lord told me, *"Corey, Jeremiah isn't just the weeping prophet: He's the man that got caught up in the heart of the Weeping God."*

The Weeping God, this simple phrase revolutionized my view of God. While reading and meditating in the book of Jeremiah, I began to get delivered from the view of God as a stoic, disconnected, faraway God, and I began to connect to the deep emotions of a God who feels, who longs, who weeps—a God who is looking for friends to weep through.

The revelation of the Weeping God opened me up to receive God as Judge. I could feel His pain, His love, and His deep compassion even while He was about to judge His people and remove them from the land. Through Jeremiah's tears, I saw the Bridegroom God whose jealousy and zeal refused to sit idly by while His wife ran to other lovers. It was in this book that I saw the vulnerability of God, the emotions of God, and I could feel His heart for me and my generation.

I came out of this season with a longing to name our next child *Jeremiah*. We quickly got pregnant, and I got very excited that Jeremiah was coming. My wife, Dana, went through two ultrasounds, but we were unable to see the sex of our baby. I was still convinced we were having a boy named *Jeremiah*.

On March 4, 2003, our baby was born, and to our surprise, she was a girl! I was blown away, and we quickly made the decision to knock off "Jere" and name her *Miah*. (We ended up spelling her name *Mya*.) She represents this whole season, and she carries the spirit and heart of the compassionate prophetess.

Right before she was born, the Lord was bringing me deeper into this place of friendship and partnership with Him. For years, I had cried out to God to wake me up in the middle of the night so that I could wrestle in intercession with Him for breakthrough in the nations. I so desperately wanted this, but there was one problem: I slept every night like a rock, and it was almost impossible to wake me up.

I'll never forget the first early morning when at three, while fully asleep, I was suddenly awakened. I was lying on my side with my face facing the wall. I knew the Lord was there, but I couldn't see Him. Yet I could hear His voice. He said softly, but firmly, "Corey, get up and be with Me." I knew it was God, and I heard Him so clearly, but I didn't want to get up. Let me rephrase that: *I* wanted to get up, but *my body* didn't. I was tired and quickly fell back to sleep.

About five minutes later, I was awakened again. "Corey, get up and be with Me." The Lord was urging me a little more strongly this time. Again, everything inside of me knew it was God who was speaking to me, yet I was unable to get up because of how tired I was. I fell asleep.

Another five minutes or so went by, and I was awakened again, "Can you not tarry with Me for one hour?" From His tone and language, I knew that I would be in trouble if I did not get up and be with Him.

I walked into Mya's room that we had prepared for her arrival and sat down in the recliner with my notepad, Bible, and pen and said, "Lord, here I am. What do You want to share with me?" I sat in that recliner for the next twenty minutes, praying in tongues, just searching for anything that I could hear Him say to me, but I heard nothing. I felt nothing. After thirty minutes of absolutely nothing, I just gave up and went back to bed.

I woke up several hours later and went to the IHOP prayer room. I was frustrated with myself for missing this opportunity. I knew it was the Lord. I understood He was answering my prayer to pray through the night, but I had failed miserably. After a couple of hours of sulking in the prayer room, I went up to a friend of mine whose knowledge and understanding of the deeper prayer life I respected. I told her what had happened and then asked her, "What do you think He wanted to tell me?"

She sat there and smiled. And then she blew my mind, *"He didn't want to tell you anything. He just wanted you to be up with Him because He was up. Corey, He calls you a friend, and a friend loves at all times."* This simple yet profound statement revolutionized my life.

As I've thought about this statement over the years, I can't help but realize that Jesus was doing to me what He did to His disciples many years before. When they were with Him in the Garden of Gethsemane, He wanted them to be up with Him on that dark night. It was in the garden where Jesus brought His three "intimates." The Bible tells us,

> Then Jesus came with them to a place called Gethsemane, and said to the disciples, "Sit here while I go and pray over there." And He took with Him *Peter and the two sons of Zebedee, and He began to be sorrowful and deeply distressed.* Then He said to them, "My soul is exceedingly sorrowful, even to death. Stay here and watch with Me."
>
> — MATTHEW 26:36–38

Three of the disciples saw a side of Jesus that the other nine did not see as Jesus didn't show this side of Himself to *all* of His disciples. These three friends saw great sorrow and deep distress consuming Jesus. In Jesus' excruciating sorrow of carrying the weight of the world on His heart, and submitting His will to the Father's will, He wanted these three young men to stay awake with Him and watch with Him. He came back two more times and found them sleeping each time.

Here's the question that baffles me: How could Peter, James, and John help alleviate Jesus' sorrow by staying up with Him and praying? What were they adding to the equation? Could it be that their staying awake and being with Jesus during that dark night actually brought comfort to Him?

I'm convinced we have no clue what it means to be friends with Jesus. There's something much more to it than we realize.

Peter's Tears

Being friends with Jesus means loving Him. It means talking to Him. It means listening to Him. It means staying up with Him. Being friends with Jesus often means standing with Him at difficult times and in hard situations. Sometimes, we blow it as Peter, James, and John did in the garden. We don't watch and pray. Instead, we sleep, or we deny. That's what Peter did, anyway.

Luke 22:54 tells us that, after Jesus' arrest, "Peter followed at a distance." And three times, individuals tried to accuse Peter of having been with Jesus, but Peter denied it each time. That's when we read, "So he went out and wept bitterly" (Luke 22:62).

Have you ever failed God miserably? Have you ever discovered that you're not as dedicated as you thought you were?

I know what it's like to come face to face with my own failure. I know Peter's tears well. I know what it feels like to experience such nearness to Jesus and intimacy with Him only to discover that I'm not as strong or dedicated as I thought I was.

I believe there are many who in the last season came face to face with the revelation of their failure. For a while, they felt disqualified, thinking their every aspiration of ever being used by God was finished. This was exactly what Peter felt. The one who had been brought into Jesus' inner circle and witnessed things only a few witnessed—like Jesus' transfiguration—was the same man who had declared Jesus as "the Christ of God" (Luke 9:20). And he was the same man who buckled three times in one night and denied being with his friend.

The pain of this kept Peter from making it to the cross. For three days, he probably battled tooth and nail through every tormenting, accusing spirit that the devil could throw his way. But there was only one reason why Peter made it through that dark night: Jesus' prayers for him. Remember Jesus' prescient words to Peter just before predicting Peter's denial?

> And the Lord said, "Simon, Simon! Indeed, Satan has asked for you, that he may sift you as wheat. But I have prayed for you, that your faith should not fail; and when you have returned to Me, strengthen your brethren."
>
> — LUKE 22:31–32

Friend, the very fact you are reading this book right now is proof of Jesus' prayer for you. His prayer carried you through your darkest nights, and this is not the end of your story.

There is a restoration day coming soon. There's a day when your tears will become a message.

We witness this in the life of the apostle Peter. Fifty days after weeping bitterly, the Lord took Peter's tears and formed the first apostolic message of the Church through him. Three thousand people were cut to the heart on the day of Pentecost, and they gave their lives to Jesus in response to Peter's message. Beloved, we need Peters whose tears of past failure have become the message of hope and deliverance for us today.

Paul's Tears

Another apostolic messenger was a weeper. Recently, after having walked through Paul's Epistles, I've been freshly marked with the heart of this man and his weeping intercessory labor for his fledgling congregations as well as his fellow countrymen.

In 2 Corinthians 11:28, Paul wrote, "What comes upon me daily" is "my deep concern for *all* the churches." Daily, he was concerned. Daily, he cared. Daily, he thought about the churches. Daily, he prayed for them and wept over them. These churches filled with immature, weak believers were his constant concern and deep burden. He carried these people in his heart like his little children, and he continually travailed in prayer and agonized in intercession for Christ to be formed in them (see Gal. 4:19).

Paul's entire life was marked by tears. His writings were filled with tears, and his warnings and pleadings were filled with tears (see Acts 20; Phil. 3:18). This kind of brokenness will be restored to church leaders!

Paul's tireless labor among the Gentiles was fueled by the crushing burden that he carried for the salvation of Israel. In Romans 9, Paul opened his heart and gave what I believe is the apostolic burden that is to mark every generation leading up to the return of the Lord: "great sorrow and continual grief" over the spiritual condition of God's people and Paul's fellow countrymen (v. 2). Paul even said, "For I could wish that I myself were accursed from Christ for my brethren, my countrymen according to the flesh, who are Israelites" (vv. 3–4).

Great sorrow and continual grief are going to come upon the Church in these last days as we share in the sufferings of our Lord for His beloved Israel. It will be this spirit resting on the Church that will provoke Israel to jealousy unto her receiving Jesus as her Messiah.

Paul's tears and labor for these young churches and for the lost was what distinguished his leadership. His "weeping" leadership is what is needed today. In fact, I believe that God is redefining the apostolic ministry in our day. He's wrecking the glorified CEO-style practice and resurrecting the truly apostolic, weeping, fathering ministry. The sole joy of weeping prophets and apostles will be sons and daughters entering into their divine destinies.

One of the hallmarks of true apostolic ministry is tears. The tears of apostles and prophets are the tears of fathers or mothers who carry sons and daughters in their hearts, in their prayers, in their labor, in their rebukes. The hearts of apostles long to protect and cover their children, keeping them from wolves and the enemy.

A New Breed of Prophets and Apostles

I believe that God is raising up prophets in the earth who will do more than just give secrets about people. I'm grateful for words of knowledge. They've greatly impacted and strengthened me, but I believe the urgent need of the day is a new breed of prophets who will prophesy the secrets of God's heart, mind, and will from the place of intimate friendship with God. I declare that weeping apostles will arise as well. These will be those who labor in travail until Christ is formed in this generation. These apostles and prophets will also do more than just speak words, but I believe they will *weep words*.

I'm convinced the only thing that will cut through the dullness, indifference, and callousness of this generation is a messenger who weeps as he or she speaks. We need weeping messengers. The billboards, T-shirts, and bumper stickers aren't going to break through the walled-up hearts of people. *We desperately need tears.*

We've gone too long with too many dry-eyed, clean-cut, polished, articulate, and attractive communicators. They say all the right words. They have all the perfect sermons, but where are their tears?

We need a new generation of prophetic messengers who speak from hearts that have been deeply cut by the words they speak. We need messengers who have stayed up and wept with Jesus. We must have apostles who have wept with the Weeping God, whose hearts have been weighted with concern for the Church, Israel, and the nations. We need broken messengers.

I'll never forget a statement made by English Christian Evangelist Leonard Ravenhill, and it's needed more today than ever before: *"It takes broken men to break men."*[1] We need messengers who are actually cut and wounded instead of having it all together—messengers who are broken. These are the messengers the Church is desperate for, and we need them by the thousands!

6

"JUST KEEP WEEPING"

MY NEXT ENCOUNTER WITH THE GIFT OF TEARS came on the heels of one of the greatest seasons I had ever been a part of, as far as a corporate move of the Holy Spirit was concerned. On November 11, 2009, the Holy Spirit broke into IHOP's Bible school in Kansas City, and within the next ten months, we saw over 7,000 testimonies of salvation, healing, and deliverance as God absolutely wrecked us in His glory.

As that awakening season ended, we began to feel a shift into a new season. The new season felt very different than the one before it. In fact, one of the leaders of that season, my dear friend Allen Hood, began to experience a physical breakdown in his body. The two of us were scheduled to minister at a conference in Fredericksburg, Virginia, around this time. As soon as we arrived at our hotel, we began to open up about our shared sense of increased warfare in our minds, bodies, and souls. Late into the evening, we talked together, wept together, and prayed together. Before we went to sleep, we asked God to speak to us, to help make sense of what we were feeling.

During that night, Allen had a profound dream that has proven to be one of the clearest prophetic navigators for us over these last nine years.

Prior to the event, Allen had written an article titled, "Standing at a Critical Juncture," for *Ministry Today*. The article looked at the book of Joel as it pertained to calling the nations to gather for prayer, fasting, and repentance. Allen emphasized that, if we did not discern the hour in which we lived, something dire—worse than our present situation—would come.

In the dream, Allen was looking on a computer screen and was reading that same article he had written. He was scrolling down to the comment boxes below the article and was shocked as he saw that the comments were from witches and warlocks who were cursing leaders, their families, and their ministries. He then clicked on one of the boxes and was nightmarishly sucked into the box. The next thing Allen knew, he was in a room facing a warlock with a python hanging from the warlock's neck. Allen looked around and saw pornography all over the back wall. He heard this man cursing him when he suddenly heard a voice behind him, saying, "Allen, it's witchcraft." (Allen later said that he hadn't ever thought of witchcraft as being connected to a real person but was more of an ethereal spirit that was out there, showing up from time to time.)

In the next scene of the dream, Allen saw thousands upon thousands of young people gathered together in a revival atmosphere, and he knew that this represented the harvest. He knew that these were the days that we had believed for and understood a great day of visitation was indeed coming. On the heels of that, Allen saw Bob Jones and I embrace one another. Then, in the dream, Bob and I declared a line out of Psalm 126:3, *"The Lord has done great things for us."*

It's important, here, to give a little background on Bob Jones as it relates to the story. Bob was a prophetic man who had a near death experience in 1975. God sent him back to prepare some end-time leaders for what was coming on the earth. One of the leaders to whom God sent him was Mike Bickle in Kansas City, Missouri.

God used Bob in profound ways during the majority of the 1980s. More specifically, Bob was used in establishing and confirming what God was going to do in Kansas City through Mike's ministry and what later would become IHOP.

Allen and I had sat in meetings with Mike for nearly twenty years, hearing story after story of how God used Bob Jones in supernatural ways to confirm what God would be doing in the coming days. Though we had never met Bob, we knew that we were deeply connected to him and knew that, in some ways, we were walking in the fulfillment of what Bob had seen.

So, for Allen to have a dream where I'm embracing Bob Jones and declaring Psalm 126, we knew that God was uniting the previous generation that saw the move of God and this generation that would experience the move of God.

"Witchcraft Has Come Against You"

After hearing Bob and I declare, *"The Lord has done great things for us,"* Allen woke up from his dream. He was very excited because the Lord had spoken in response to our prayer.

Even though Allen saw the warfare was witchcraft and we needed to war, he was relieved because at least he knew what it was we were standing against and where it was leading. (Knowing what's going on is 75 percent of the battle.)

Allen quickly came to my hotel room, knocked on my door, and said emphatically, "Get ready and meet me down at breakfast. The Lord has spoken to me."

I got ready as fast as I could and went downstairs to join him. As soon as he saw me, Allen began to tell me the dream. While he was telling me the part of the dream where Bob Jones and I embraced, a random lady came up and interrupted Allen, "Are you Allen Hood?"

"Yes, I am," Allen responded, a bit surprised.

She then said, "Hi, my name is Bonnie Jones, and my husband, Bob, and I would like to have breakfast with you two."

We were absolutely floored! Bob Jones was sitting at a table near us, and we had no clue. We had no clue that he would be anywhere near Virginia, so we knew that God was up to something. And here was his wife, sent to our table to invite us to sit with them. "O-Okay," we said as we followed her to their table in complete shock and awe. We were going to meet the man about whom we had been hearing stories for nearly the past twenty years—the very man who was a key figure in Allen's dream only the night before.

When we sat down, the first thing I asked Bob Jones was where in Arkansas he was from. "I'm from Waldron," he said.

"Well, I'm from Alma," I said. Unbelievable! The man was from a city about thirty to forty minutes from where I was born and raised.

For the next hour and a half, Bob spoke about many cryptic things, and Allen and I were both doing our best to hang on, trying to interpret what some of Bob's phrases meant and how they applied to our current situation. Honestly, we didn't understand most of what he was talking about. Prophetic seer types see things and try to voice what it is they're seeing, leaving many of us lost in wonder. But I've discovered that, when you're in a situation like this, you just need to shake your head up and down, looking penetratingly at the prophet, and it will go a long way.

Toward the end of our time, he began to talk with more clarity, or I should say Allen and I were finally getting the interpretation. Bob shared how for years he was praying and hoping that our nation could get revival without judgment, but that now he was convinced both would be coming. Our nation would see both revival and judgment. At this point, he began to prophesy over us, and the words that came out of his mouth would shape and give definition to the next nine years of our lives.

"You boys have been preaching Joel," Bob said, "and you've been calling the Church to prayer and fasting, and I see that witchcraft has come against you." He then looked over at me and said, "I see python marks in your neck."

He then continued on with talking about the warfare surrounding calling the Church to prayer and fasting and how witchcraft had been released against leaders standing for these two sacred acts.

Allen had heard stories of how certain leaders in the Body of Christ in the past had been under warfare and Bob had prayed for them, which resulted in their being supernaturally delivered. So, Allen decided to ask Bob, "Would you pray for us to break this off?"

"I ain't gonna do that religious thing," Bob quickly retorted. "What do you think I've been doing for the last two hours?"

We looked at each other and thought to ourselves, *Talking*, but we didn't dare say that to him.

He then followed up with, "You boys have been weeping, haven't you?"

We nodded our heads up and down like two little school-boys answering the principal. We were remembering how the previous night we had wept together.

Bob looked us in the eyes and gave us one of the most profound insights we would ever receive. "You boys see, witchcraft gets in your eyes, and it makes you look on your past seasons as if you've never done anything for God. Then it makes you look on future seasons and makes you think that you'll never do anything for God . . . but weeping gets the witchcraft out of your eyes. You boys are going to be fine. Your ministries are good. *Just keep weeping.*"

Those words, *"Just keep weeping,"* seemed to keep repeating over and over again as we sat there with our mouths hanging open, blown away with the prophetic accuracy that just gave definition to things that we really had no clue we would be walking into.

Friend, no doubt you have been through similar seasons where you looked back on past seasons wondering if you've ever done anything for God and you've looked on future seasons wondering if you will ever do anything for God. I want to speak to you what Bob spoke to us: *"Just keep weeping."*

Little did we know, within the next two years, Allen's body would enter into a thyroid storm, affecting many parts of his physical, mental, and emotional makeup. And the tragedy of tragedies would strike at my family when my youngest child, my only son, would be laid down for a nap at nine and a half months old but would never wake up in this life. It has been eight years, at the time of this writing, since my son passed. The earthquake that has been released in our family has been intense. There has been a lot of weeping.

There were countless times over the last eight years when I couldn't do anything but weep and weep and weep. At those times, I could hear Bob say, "You boys are going to be fine. . . . Just keep weeping." This little phrase carried me through some dark nights when I couldn't see anything at all.

Cleansing the Eyes

In such times, I've learned tears precede revelation. When we have exhausted every human solution—when there are no other options as we've hit a place of emptiness and desperation—tears come, our eyes are cleansed, and revelation of Jesus follows. We begin to see Him in a new way.

Like John the beloved apostle in the book of Revelation, his weeping preceded the revelation of the Slain Lamb amid the throne, living creatures, and elders. We read:

And I saw in the right hand of Him who sat on the throne a scroll written inside and on the back, sealed with seven seals. Then I saw a strong angel proclaiming with a loud voice, "Who is worthy to open the scroll and to loose its seals?" And no one in heaven or on the earth or under the earth was able to open the scroll, or to look at it. So *I wept much,* because no one was found worthy to open and read the scroll, or to look at it. But one of the elders said to me, "Do not weep. Behold, the Lion of the tribe of Judah, the Root of David, has prevailed to open the scroll and to loose its seven seals." And I looked, and behold, in the midst of the throne and of the four living creatures, and in the midst of the elders, stood a Lamb as though it had been slain, having seven horns and seven eyes, which are the seven Spirits of God sent out into all the earth.

— REVELATION 5:1–6

John heard that there wasn't one person who could open the scroll and loose its seals. What was it about this that caused John to weep so much?

The core reason John wept was, since there was no one to open and loose the seals, then injustice, wickedness, and sin would continue in the earth—and would continue unchecked. The ravaging effects of sin would go on, and humanity would continue to tumble into the depths of depravity.

At his lowest place in weeping, an elder came up to John and told him to stop. What Heaven had started in John Heaven stopped in John as he was told by the elder there was One who was found worthy.

We are familiar with what happens next as John beheld the Slain Lamb take the scroll and a new song erupt in Heaven. But let's not miss something very striking in the text: *Weeping preceded seeing.*

The cleansing of the eyes through tears prepared John to see the Slain Lamb with seven horns and seven eyes.

I believe God is going to bring this next generation of messengers through similar doors of weeping to prepare them for beholding and then proclaiming the Lamb of God in all of His glory and majesty. I believe this is what many of those in Kingdom ministry have been experiencing in these last days.

The Weeping Psalm

I've found that these last several years have been some of the most intense for many of those who have been on the front-lines for the Kingdom. Many of my friends across the earth have gone through their own bone-crushing season where every fault line was exposed in their lives, marriages, and families. These all have been brought to a place of weeping, groaning, and clinging.

These are the moments of severe trial, and it's in these seasons when tears are all you have. You don't know what to say, what to pray, or what to sing, but you have tears. I believe what I found hidden in Allen's dream was the line out of Psalm 126, which is called "The Weeping Psalm." The psalm reads:

When the Lord brought back the captivity of Zion, we were like those who dream. Then our mouth was filled with laughter, and our tongue with singing. Then they said among the nations, "The Lord has done great things for them." The Lord has done great things for us, and we are glad. Bring back our captivity, O Lord, as the streams in the South. Those who sow in tears shall reap in joy. He who continually goes forth weeping, bearing seed for sowing, shall doubtless come again with rejoicing, bringing his sheaves with him.

The current weeping, groaning, and travailing that you may have endured in the last season are leading you to a season of promise, harvest, joy, dreaming, and singing.

Many in the Church have been in captivity in the last season. Marriages have been in captivity, children in captivity, ministries in captivity. Some have been in captivity because of their own sin and rebellion, and they are under the discipline of God. Others are in captivity like Joseph and are under the rage of Satan. Whether your captivity is a result your own decisions or not, the same thing is being worked in you in this season. Weeping. Groaning. Humility.

The same pride, arrogance, self-confidence, and harshness have been replaced with brokenness, humility, tenderness, compassion, and the deep knowledge of your need for the Lord and that apart from Him you are nothing.

This season of bone crushing has produced the choicest seed that brings forth the choicest harvest: tears.

The Greatest Weepers Will Become the Greatest Reapers

The psalmist lets us know tears are seeds, and they are being sown into the ground (see Ps. 126:6). These tears are living and will bring forth something glorious in the next season. The tears you are sowing in this season will come forth in joy in the next season.

The water flowing from your eyes in this season will be turned into joy. Singing and rejoicing will fill your next season.

The water flowing from your eyes will be turned into wine. He stores your tears in His bottle and not one tear will be wasted.

Laughter is coming, friend.

Dreaming again is coming, friend.

Singing is coming again, friend.

Harvest is coming, friend.

I cannot adequately communicate how impactful this encounter with Bob Jones was for me and the power of Psalm 126 over these last several years has been in my life. In some of my darkest moments and hours, I could hear Bob saying, "You boys are going to be okay. Your ministries are good." This would stabilize my heart, knowing that there was an end coming to this season and having the assurance that the end would be great joy in declaring, *"The Lord has done great things for us."*

7

TEARS IN A BOTTLE

IN JULY 2018, DANA AND I TOOK OUR ELDEST daughter to a mission school in Colorado Springs. The entire week leading up to her departure was very difficult, but the weekend we actually took her to school was off-the-charts as we were experiencing all the anxious emotions of sending our firstborn off into the world. Feeling the weight of it all, wanting to make sure she had everything she needed from us for her to thrive in her new environment, I went to pray the morning we were sending her to school. I wanted God to break through it all in her heart and in our hearts as well. I began to pray in the Spirit about thirty minutes before we would be dropping her off. I desperately needed God to speak. And He did, only moments before we would leave.

"Put my tears into your bottle." In one moment, I heard that phrase, and then I saw in my mind's eye about four or five times over the past twenty years where I had gut-level, ugly crying sessions with God for our daughter. As all parents

know, there are those seasons where the enemy seeks to take out our kids, and we must cry out for God to spare them and pull them through. I remembered those times that day.

After those scenes passed through my mind, I heard a simple whisper from the Lord: *"Corey, I've got her."* Now, when I heard that phrase, every fear, anxiety, and swirl of emotion immediately dissolved, and a great peace and joy suddenly flooded my soul.

Quickly, I grabbed my Bible and began to look for that phrase. I knew it was a Bible verse, but I didn't know where it was. I finally found it in Psalm 56:8.

> You number my wanderings, put my tears into Your bottle; are they not in your book?

This prayer by David is so profound, and it gives me such confidence knowing that every season I walk through is seen by God and He brings forth His purpose for every season.

Stored Tears and Numbered Wanderings

When I first began to walk with the Lord, I just assumed that my walk would be a steady incline over the years, culminating with my arrival at this place of ecstasy and intimacy with God. What I've come to find out, though, is that there are *many* seasons where it seems as if I'm going backward and sideways, I'm stopped and then sitting on the sidelines, and finally I'm moving forward.

What blows me away is that God uses all of these twists and turns in our story to bring us into fullness with deep humility and gratitude. God used David's wanderings from Him, to Him, away from Him, to the Philistines, to the throne, to the failures after the throne, and to Solomon to drive home one big point: *He uses it all.*

God has a bottle, and God has a book. God takes account of every prayer, tear, groan, and whisper, and stores them—He stores everything! I believe that He stores all of these in this age for the purpose of divine seasons when He pours them out through salvation, deliverance, and restoration. I also believe that God stores our tears, and they are related to rewards in the age to come.

In Revelation 5, we see there will come a day when bowls in Heaven will be full of the prayers of the saints: "Golden *bowls full* of incense, which are *the prayers* of the saints" (v. 8). Later in Revelation 8, we read, "And the smoke of the incense, with the prayers of the saints, ascended before God *from the angel's hand*" (v. 4). God will take full bowls of prayers to bring forth His purpose in the earth. I believe the same regarding this bottle David mentioned in Psalm 56:8.

"Put my tears into Your bottle," David prayed. I can't help but think of David as an investor who was asking God to take his tears and invest them into a stock that would never stop yielding amazing returns for eternity.

Friend, our tears live forever before God. God stores these tears, and they serve as catalysts and agents in seeing God's deliverance, salvation, and breakthrough in our lives and in the lives of others.

God doesn't waste one tear. Every tear you've forgotten crying will never be forgotten by God but is used in His economy. I want you to hear that. God stores every one of your tears in a bottle in Heaven, and in the divine time and season, He pours that bottle out into your life, your family, your circumstances, your world.

If you're a parent, I believe you have cried many tears for your children. You have wept and wept for their salvation, deliverance, healing, and protection, and I want you to hear the Lord saying to you, "I've stored every one of your tears in My bottle."

Friend, He's going to turn your water into wine. He's going to turn your places of greatest pain into places of greatest joy.

Joseph's Tears

I believe that we are going to see tears of restoration happen in families in this next season. Family members who have been estranged for decades are going to see glorious reunions in this coming season.

A few years ago, I had a dream where I was standing in front of a large group, and I was telling the people to turn to Psalm 105, but I couldn't find Psalm 105 in my Bible. I spent the rest of the dream looking for Psalm 105 without being able to find it.

When I woke up, I felt the urgency to find Psalm 105 in my Bible, and then I immediately gave myself to the chapter. In fact, I spent a couple months reading, meditating, and studying through this psalm.

The main thing that stood out to me in the psalm was the story of Joseph and how he was tested:

He sent a man before them—Joseph—who was sold as a slave. They hurt his feet with fetters, he was laid in irons. Until the time that his word came to pass, the word of the Lord tested him.

— PSALM 105:17–19

There are few stories that are better in the Bible than the story of Joseph's life. An entire book could be written examining his story, the betrayal of his brothers, and the journey to their reunion in Egypt. I could pull out so many principles, but for our purposes here, I want to look at what happened when Joseph revealed himself to his brothers in the Genesis account.

Then Joseph could not restrain himself before all those who stood by him, and cried out, "Make everyone go out from me!" So no one stood with him while Joseph made himself known to his brothers. *And he wept aloud,* and the Egyptians and the house of Pharaoh heard it.

— GENESIS 45:1–2

I believe this moment is a prophetic picture of what it will look like when Jesus is revealed as Israel's Messiah at His return. The "One" whom the brothers sold into slavery is the "One" who will save them in a coming famine and tribulation on the earth. In the same way Joseph's brothers didn't recognize him the first time they came to Egypt, but it was the second time that he revealed himself to them, so Israel did not recognize Jesus at His first coming, but the whole nation will recognize and receive Him as their Messiah at His second coming.

They will weep and weep and weep as they see the One whom they had pierced is their Messiah:

> "And I will pour on the house of David and on the inhabitants of Jerusalem the Spirit of grace and supplication; then they will look on Me whom they pierced. Yes, they will mourn for Him as one mourns for his only son, and grieve for Him as one grieves for a firstborn."
>
> — ZECHARIAH 12:10

The brothers will be restored. The family will be restored, and all Israel will be saved.

I want to encourage you. You may have broken relationships with family members that have spanned years and decades even. Betrayal, hatred, jealousy, competition, comparison, and favoritism may have divided you from your siblings, your parents, your loved ones. Perhaps you continued to walk forward in your life, but there was a deep pain that you've carried for years.

In the same way God had to work out any anger, vindictive nature on the inside of Joseph, and bring him to a rest and confidence—in the same way that God set the whole thing up for Joseph and his brothers—I believe that He's been doing the same thing in you and your loved ones for the purpose of your family's destiny.

"What you meant for evil, God meant it for good" will become your mantra (see Gen. 50:20).

I believe that tears of reconciliation are going to be released in this next season. I believe these reunions will restore and redeem many years, and it will leave a lasting impact on your children.

Friend, God has stored your tears in His bottle and numbered your wanderings in His book. He has every intention of working it all for your good. He has every intention of assuring you, "I've got her. I've got him. I've got you." He will bring His purposes to pass through your tears.

8

CORPORATE TEARS

Up until this point, we've shared on the power of tears in the lives of individuals, and there are so many amazing examples of this. In this chapter, I want to look at the power of corporate tears. I've found in my journey that I experience a level of breakthrough when I reach a place of desperation, but when a company of people who have developed a history together in God reach a place of desperation together, the floodgates of Heaven open, and God ushers in times and seasons of His manifest Presence. I believe we're going to experience this in the coming days.

We are in an urgent hour in the earth. I believe we are at the forefront of the generation of the Lord's return, and I'm convinced that the only way to navigate the coming days will be through a corporate people who have broken through into the weeping room together.

Psalm 2 Crisis

Psalm 2 may be the most prophetic twelve verses in all of Scripture, pointing to where we are currently at in the world, in our nation, and in this generation. David, who wrote this psalm, was in a full-on vision and was seeing something unprecedented, something global, and something demonic. I'm utterly convinced that we are at the beginning of what David was seeing in Psalm 2.

David was witnessing a time in history when insanity and rebellion reach a level where people at the highest positions of influence are in unity against the same Person: the Father and the Son. He wrote:

> Why do the nations rage, and the people plot a vain thing? The kings of the earth set themselves, and the rulers take counsel together, against the Lord and against His Anointed saying, "Let us break Their bonds in pieces and cast away Their cords from us."
>
> — PSALM 2:1–3

David was seeing an hour where a generation openly and boldly declared, "We don't have to repent for our sin. We can celebrate it!" David, like us, felt these days increasing around him. Our temptation is toward anxiety, fear, and desire to stop it by openly declaring, *"No! Why would you do this?"*

I believe God wants us to feel the encroaching darkness, but He doesn't want us to engage in the battle from the ground level. The Father is inviting us to the throne room to gain His perspective and to be filled with His confidence as He addresses the same dynamic yet in a different way:

> He who sits in the heavens shall laugh; the Lord shall hold them in derision. Then He shall speak to them in His wrath, and distress them in His deep displeasure: "Yet I have set My King on My holy hill of Zion."
>
> — PSALM 2:4–6

The Father wants to fill His people with His confidence— with His laugh. This verse is terrifying as we see the Father openly stirs up the nations to do what is in their hearts but makes a very strong and bold statement to them: "We've already voted on who gets to be King and the land He will rule, and you weren't in the voting process. And you're definitely not a candidate!" The Father is going to exalt His Son openly in the eyes of the nations through the Church across the earth and through His return to the planet. I could literally walk through every verse in this glorious psalm, but I want to get to the response that I believe is so necessary in these days.

A Joel 2 Response: Corporate Weeping

In chapter five, the very source of the demonic warfare we experienced was around the message of Joel, which was what Allen Hood had discussed in the article he had written and then dreamed about. I'm convinced that the book of Joel is a key for the Church in these days.

We've talked about individuals who weep and the power such weeping possesses. But I believe God is taking us to corporate weeping, and this is what Joel's response is all about.

The prophet Joel showed up in chapter 1, pretty much unannounced on the back end of a four-wave locust plague that had completely destroyed Israel's economy and thereby the nation. Joel was well aware of what God had spoken to Solomon at the dedication of the temple, where God had said,

> When I shut up heaven and there is no rain, or command the locusts to devour the land, or send pestilence among My people, if My people who are called by My name will humble themselves, and pray and seek My face, and turn from their wicked ways, then I will hear from heaven, and will forgive their land.
>
> — 2 CHRONICLES 7:13–14

The locust swarms were clear signs to call the people to turn, humble themselves, and seek God, and then the Lord would have mercy. So, in the very first chapter of Joel, the prophet called the entire nation to prayer and fasting.

In chapter 2, Joel began to look toward the future and in essence said, "If you guys don't hear what God is saying through the locust plague, there is something far worse that is coming. It's military invasion." Joel laid out in detail the characteristics of this army, and in light of it called the people to turn in their hearts to God and make fresh "eye contact" with Him. *At the end of the day, all that God is ever longing for is a sincere shift of the heart to Him and an urgency in doing it.*

In the middle of this intense chapter, we find what I believe is the most powerful verses in the book and, in my opinion, one of the most prophetic words to the Church in this hour,

> "Now, therefore," says the Lord, "turn to Me with all your heart, with fasting, with weeping and with mourning. So rend your heart, and not your garments; return to the Lord your God, for He is gracious and merciful, slow to anger, and of great kindness; and He relents from doing harm."
>
> — JOEL 2:12–13

I want to slow down right here, and I want you to feel this verse. I sense such compassion in a Father who is looking at a son who is about to undergo a difficult situation, and with tears in His eyes, says, "Now. . . ." In essence, the Father is saying, "Don't put this off for another day. I want your eye contact. I want your attention. I want your heart, and I know it's been a while since you've done this."

The Father continues by saying that He is giving three gifts to get us into contact with our hearts: fasting, tears, and mourning. I'm convinced that these three same gifts are being released to the Church in these days. These gifts are going to release a tenderness and release a rending of the heart to respond to God from the depths of our being.

Joel first dealt with the individual call, and then he set his sights on the corporate call to weeping.

> "Blow the trumpet in Zion, consecrate a fast, call a sacred assembly; gather the people, . . . gather the children and nursing babes. . . . Let the priests, who minister to the Lord, weep between the porch and the altar; let them say, 'Spare your people, O Lord!'"

> — JOEL 2:15–17

The only way to deal with corporate insanity is by corporate gatherings of prayer and fasting. I'm grateful for building my individual prayer life, but the only way forward is for us to forge histories of vulnerable seeking after God together. Hebrews 10:25 tells us not to forsake the assembling of ourselves together as the Day approaches. A fuller dimension is experienced corporately that isn't experienced individually. I believe corporate humility, brokenness, and weeping will provoke a corporate outpouring of the Spirit.

As we've learned from Mary of Bethany, there is something about sincere weeping before God that moves Him deeply. I'm convinced that the devil's main warfare is over keeping the book of Joel off the minds of believers because in it contains the response that God is looking for. I'm convinced that the devil will let us build big ministries, have big meetings, and accrue big bank accounts, but people who call others to build corporate histories of prayer, fasting, and weeping will be on the devil's hit list because it's this kind of stuff that shakes the foundations of nations.

As we've already discussed, apostolic and prophetic leaders who weep and lead others in weeping are the greatest need of the day, leaders who don't strut in their own strength but live on their knees in dependence on God. Leaders who have eyes filled with tears, hearts that are tender, and words that are born from above are needed today.

Acts 2 Outpouring

What does God do when His people do Joel 2?

> When the Day of Pentecost had fully come, they were all with one accord in one place. And suddenly there came a sound from heaven, as of a rushing mighty wind, and it filled the whole house where they were sitting. Then there appeared to them divided tongues, as of fire, and one sat upon each of them. And they were all filled with the Holy Spirit and began to speak with other tongues, as the Spirit gave them utterance.
>
> — ACTS 2:1–4

> But Peter, standing up with the eleven, raised his voice and said to them. . . . "This is what was spoken by the prophet Joel: 'And it shall come to pass in the last days, says God, that I will pour out of My Spirit on all flesh. . . . *before* the coming of the great and awesome day of the Lord.'"
>
> — ACTS 2:14, 16–17, 20

When God finds a corporate people who have rent their hearts and who lead by weeping, and He finds leaders who have joined together in prayer and fasting and cried out to Him for His Spirit, He shows up.

Of all the prophets Peter could have chosen to highlight on the Day of Pentecost, he chose Joel. There were similar prophecies from Isaiah and Ezekiel, yet he chose a little, three-chapter minor prophet named Joel. I'm convinced it's because Joel gave us the clearest response of what to do in tumultuous days. When Peter declared that "this is that," he was proclaiming Joel's prophecy had begun and would continue until the coming of the great Day of the Lord. Joel gives us clarity on what to do when rage, chaos, and confusion are the norm, and he made it very clear what God would do: *He would pour out His Spirit.*

We are being prepared for the greatest revival the earth has ever seen. When I talk about revival, I am talking about those sovereign seasons when God openly manifests the rule and reign of His Son by the outpouring of the Holy Spirit and apostolic preaching which, in short, is preaching that cuts.

We've seen times and seasons throughout history when the culture was at all-time lows and cities, regions, and nations were anti-God. Yet, in such times, God finds a people who will seek Him, and then He comes down. We have had great awakenings in our own nation when God came down. We've seen the marks of what happens and how God literally changes people for eternity and cities are never the same.

We are going to see it again, friend, when God comes down and visits cities and regions with His manifest Presence

—all in response to the corporate tears and cries of His people. And His Word will go forth out of messengers who have been cut by the words they proclaim. This is what we want, and this is what we need. *Do it, Lord!*

9

REVIVAL TEARS

I'VE ALWAYS BEEN BLOWN AWAY THAT IT WAS NOT enough to begin Christianity by having a forty-day conference with Jesus in a resurrected body. We know from Scripture that Jesus had spent the forty days after His resurrection teaching on the Kingdom and preparing these young apostles for the greatest transition in human history. Having given them all that teaching, He commanded them to "wait for the Promise of the Father, 'which,' He said, 'you have heard from Me; for John truly baptized with water, but you shall be baptized with the Holy Spirit not many days from now" (Acts 1:4–5).

So, what did they do?

Peter and those 120 spent ten days in a prayer meeting, waiting. And it was their prayers, tears, groans, and travail that gave birth to that historic day when "suddenly there came a sound from heaven, as of a rushing mighty wind, and it filled the whole house where they were sitting. . . . And they were all filled with the Holy Spirit and began to speak with other tongues, as the Spirit gave them utterance" (Acts 2:2–4).

Over the last two thousand years, the Lord's command still rings out, and whenever God has found intercessors or companies of people to hear the call and give themselves to it in their generation, they have seen God invade their cities, regions, and nations with the outpouring of the Holy Spirit. Such times are what Peter called, "Times of refreshing . . . from the presence of the Lord" (Acts 3:19). This is what I call *revival*, and there is a certain kind of praying that precedes it. As we have learned in previous chapters, it's a broken, weeping kind of praying that pulls the holiest things out of God to come down and change the world.

There have been these times and seasons over the last couple thousand years when God steps down and does in a matter of weeks and months something that lasts for decades and centuries. There have been great awakenings in our nation where hundreds of thousands of souls were swept into the Kingdom in a matter of weeks.

God has always found His Jonathan Edwards, His Charles Finney, His William Seymour, or His Duncan Campbell—all well-known revivalists in their day. And He has had His lesser-known intercessors like Daniel Nash, Frank Bartleman, or Peggy and Christine Smith. Their prayers reached out from the depths of their beings and pulled out the holy things of God. Their prayers stirred His bowels and apprehended His compassion to touch a lost and broken world with His love and conviction.

One of my favorite revival intercessors is Frank Bartleman. He was an American Pentecostal writer, evangelist, and missionary who experienced and recorded the early beginnings of the Pentecostal outpouring at the start of the 1900s.

In an earlier chapter, I highlighted how, sometimes, we are brought to such desperate places of pain and brokenness in our lives that something is opened up within us. As a result, we throw our lives fully on God to see Him move. Frank Bartleman was brought to such a place at the death of his three-year-old daughter, Esther. The tears he shed over her death reignited his prayer life.

"I was staggered, stunned," by her death, the heartbroken father confessed in 1908. Despite his personal sorrow, Bartleman interpreted his little girl's death in larger cosmic terms, as God's wakeup call to prepare him to participate in the end-time revival that he believed was imminent. "My own awakening, or reawakening to this plan," he confided, "was brought about through the loss of my little girl."[1]

Here's his description of what he experienced after his daughter's death:

Little Esther's death had broken my heart, and I felt I could only live while in God's service. I longed to know Him in a more real way and to see the work of God go forth in power. A great burden and cry came in my heart for a mighty revival. He was preparing for a fresh service for Him. This could only be brought about by the realization of a deeper need in my own heart for God and a real soul travail for the work of God. This He gave me. Many were being similarly prepared at this time in different parts of the world. The

Lord was preparing to visit and deliver His people once more. Intercessors were the need.[2]

Travail is one of the hallmarks of true revival. Holy Spirit releases this intense prayer anointing in specific seasons to bring about His intended purpose. When this happens, the grace of God seems to expand the human soul, enabling it to feel more deeply and pray more earnestly. Bartleman described this as the Spirit interceding *through* him. I know several people who have experienced travail in intercession, and each would testify that it is not something they produced on their own. It takes God to pray in this way.

When not engaged in public ministry or attending services at local churches, Bartleman prayed, sometimes all night at home or in an accommodating Holiness mission. "It seemed as though I carried a nation on my heart," he was to write of these months of intense intercessory prayer before the Pentecostal outpouring.[3]

It was stories like Bartleman's that cut me very deeply many years ago. I've thought on Bartleman's intercession often since my son passed away in 2013. In times of great loss, under the weight of tremendous grief, eternity seems to bear down on your soul, possessing you with a vision to see God's Kingdom break into the earth. For me, in 2013, I was experiencing a time of favor and momentum. During the previous six years, I had written two books, released two new prayer albums, and was seeing many open doors. I was riding a wave. Looking back, however, I see where I was starting to get comfortable with a nice itinerant traveling ministry. But March 16, 2013, changed everything. More specifically, it awakened such a deep, all-consuming desire in me to see God come down.

I believe that there will be many storylines that bring God's people to a place of desperation for Him to move in our generation. The primary purpose of God is bringing you to that point. *He's bringing you to the place where you will shed tears—tears for revival. He's bringing you past the place of words to release tongues for revival. He's bringing you to the altar where you will labor with Him—where you will travail for revival.*

Bartleman realized something that I believe is important for us to understand as well. He realized that others were being prepared as he was, only they were being prepared alone in different places on the globe. Though you may be alone in your weeping room, you are not alone among weepers.

Beloved, all the tears of individuals are coming together and provoking corporate tears for revival. His Spirit will be poured out in these last days. Revival will break out all over the world. Miracles, signs, wonders, deliverances, salvations, baptisms, hearts on fire for Jesus—all of these will transpire. And I just want to shout, *"Let it all come, God!"*

10

"TRY TEARS"

WE HAVE LITERALLY TRIED EVERYTHING IN THE Church to change this generation. We have built bigger churches, bigger outreaches, bigger conferences. We have released more products, more Bibles in every translation, and we have come up with more sophisticated and polished ways to do evangelism, prophecy, and every other ministry under the sun. But have we tried tears?

Many years ago, the Salvation Army sent workers to Los Angeles to bring the gospel to some of the worst parts of the city. After laboring for three years, they sent a telegram to the founder, William Booth, letting him know that they had tried every technique and every strategy yet had seen no fruit. They asked him if they could move to another station and take on another city.

Booth sent back a telegram with a two-word response, "Try tears."

I believe that our journey into tears begins with asking for tears. You can ask God to give you tears. Jeremiah gave us a prayer for tears that I believe God wants to release upon this generation. "Oh, that my head were waters, and my eyes a fountain of tears, that I might weep day and night" (9:1).

Friend, you can ask God to make your head so full of tears that your eyes become a fountain of weeping water.

You can ask God to give you tears over a people's or a culture's resistance to His Word. You can ask Him to cause "rivers of water" to run down from your eyes "because men do not keep" His law (Ps. 119:136).

You can ask God to give you tears of repentance—bitter tears—like He gave to Hezekiah after Hezekiah heard Isaiah's prophecy of doom. Isaiah had prophesied, "Set your house in order, for you shall die, and not live" (2 Kings 20:1). But upon hearing these words, Hezekiah turned and prayed to the Lord. He "wept bitterly," and God added fifteen years to his life (2 Kings 20:3, 6).

You can ask God for Paul's tears—the tears of a weeping apostle for the churches in our day. You can ask God for tears for His people throughout the earth as they face persecution and hardship, as they suffer for the sake of the gospel of Jesus Christ.

You can ask God for the tears of Mary Magdalene—the tears of the woman who was forgiven much and loved much (see Luke 7:47). You can ask God to give you tears that wash His feet in gratitude for His great love and compassion.

Oh, God, raise up an entire generation of those who know how much they've been forgiven and who lavish Jesus with their tears, their praise, and their lives!

To preachers who are reading this, those who are in full-time ministry, or those who feel called to full-time ministry, I plead with you to try tears. The days are far gone of having more polished and articulate messages that reach the mind. We desperately need messages bathed in tears. We need messages born in the heart that can once again reach the heart of this generation. Go to your knees and ask God to give you tears. Ask Him for words to come out of your mouth that would cut through the noise of the thousands of messages being proclaimed and the millions of songs being sung every day.

I remember a story I once heard about a Scottish preacher, Robert Murray M'Cheyne. Sometime after he had passed away, an admirer of his was traveling through Scotland and came to his church. He was greeted at the door by a gentleman to whom he said, "I am very fond of Mr. M'Cheyne. I am a fan of his. I love his ministry with all my heart. Can you tell me just one secret or any secret about this man's ministry?"

The gentleman said, "Sure, come in Mr. M'Cheyne's study." He showed the admirer M'Cheyne's desk and gave him permission to go sit down at the desk. Then the gentleman told the admirer something I will never forget. He said, "Just bend over like this and put your face in your hands and let the water come. Let the tears flow." He explained that was the way M'Cheyne did it.

The gentleman walked the admirer into the sanctuary next, taking him up onto the stage and before the pulpit. He said to the admirer, "Put your elbows down, put your face in your hands. Now cry. Cry and cry your heart out. That is the way he did it, and that's why he witnessed what he witnessed."

Friend, I plead with you. Try tears.

NOTES

Foreword

1. "Uncle Tom's Cabin." Simple English Wikipedia, January 30, 2021. https://simple.wikipedia.org/wiki/Uncle_Tom%27s_Cabin/.
2. "Uncle Tom's Cabin." https://simple.wikipedia.org/wiki/Uncle_Tom%27s_Cabin/.

3. Mary's Tears

1. Alice Lady Lovat, *The Life of Saint Teresa: Taken from the French of "A Carmelite Nun"* (St. Louis, Missouri: B. Herder, 1912), 548. Teresa described her journey as follows: "'We had to run many dangers. At no part of the road were the risks greater than within a few leagues of Burgos, at a place called Los Pontes. The rivers were so high that the water in places covered everything, neither road nor the smallest foot-path could be seen, only water everywhere, and two abysses on each side. It seemed foolhardiness to advance, especially in a carriage, for if one strayed ever so little off the road (then invisible), one must have perished.' The saint is silent on her share of the adventure, but her companions relate that, seeing their alarm, she turned to them and encouraged them, saying that 'as they were engaged in doing God's work, how could they die in a better cause?' She then led the way on foot. The current was so strong that she lost her footing, and was on the point of being carried away when our Lord sustained her. 'Oh, my Lord!' she exclaimed, with her usual loving familiarity, 'when wilt Thou cease from scattering obstacles in our path?' 'Do not complain, daughter,' the Divine Master answered, 'for it is ever thus that I treat My friends.' 'Ah, Lord, it is also on that account that Thou hast so few!' was her reply."

4. "Jesus Wept"

1. Charles Haddon Spurgeon, "Jesus Wept." *The Spurgeon Center for Biblical Preaching at Midwestern Seminary,* https://www.spurgeon.org/resource-library/sermons/jesus-wept/#flipbook/. Emphasis added by author.

5. Weeping Prophets and Apostles

1. Leonard Ravenill, *Why Revival Tarries* (Minneapolis: Bethany House Publishers, 1987) 111.

9. Revival Tears

1. Augustus Cerillo Jr., "Frank Bartleman: Pentecostal 'Lone Ranger' and Social Critic," in *Portraits of a Generation: Early Pentecostal Leaders,* ed. James R. Goff Jr. and Grant Wacker (University of Arkansas Press, 2002), 109–10.
2. Frank Bartleman, *Azusa Street: The Roots of Modern-day Pentecost* (Gainesville, FL: Bridge-Logos, 1980), 9.
3. Bartleman, *Azusa Street,* 17.

ABOUT THE AUTHOR

Corey Russell's passion is to awaken the Church across the earth to the beauty of Jesus, intimacy with the Holy Spirit, and the power of prayer. He has written seven books and released five prayer albums. He and his family spent eighteen years in Kansas City, Missouri, with International House of Prayer, and he is currently on the staff of Global Upper Room based in Dallas, Texas. He has been married to his wife, Dana, for over twenty years and has three daughters and one son.

facebook.com/brotherrussell
twitter.com/brotherrussell
instagram.com/brotherrussell_

Printed in Great Britain
by Amazon

86084833R10068